Titl

The Call of Blood

John Nkemngong Nkengasong

Langaa Research & Publishing CIG
Mankon, Bamenda

Publisher:
Langaa RPCIG
Langaa Research & Publishing Common Initiative
Group
P.O. Box 902 Mankon
Bamenda
North West Region
Cameroon
Langaagrp@gmail.com
www.langaa-rpcig.net

Distributed outside N. America by African Books
Collective
orders@africanbookscollective.com
www.africanbookscollective.com

Distributed in N. America by Michigan State
University Press
msupress@msu.edu
www.msupress.msu.edu

ISBN: 9956-616-11-7

DISCLAIMER

The names, characters, places and incidents in this book are either the product of the author's imagination or are used fictitiously. Accordingly, any resemblance to actual persons, living or dead, events, or locales is entirely one of incredible coincidence.

Contents

A reading of *The Call of Blood* was done in New York City by the New York Theatre Workshop on the 17th of November, 2008.

Directed by: Rafael Gallegos

Cast

EFENZE: Erwin E.A. Thomas

MESHI: Roselyn Ruff

WANGE: Maduka Steady

MANKA: Brenda Pressley

NGANDO/
STAGE DIRECTIONS: Garrett Bantom

For all who toil for a better humanity

THE CHARACTERS

EFENZE   Meshi's husband

MESHI   Efenze's wife

WANGE   Friend to Efenze

MANKA   Sancheu's widow

NGANDO   Efenze's driver

1

ACT ONE

An elaborate bedchamber. Dim saffron lights from bedpost lamp.

Occupying a reasonable portion of the room is a bed, adjacent, a wardrobe. On the rear of the bed, Meshi is stretched out under a luxuriant counterpane. Only the faint gleam of her face is visible. She is half asleep.

Besides the wardrobe, at the foot of the bed, Efenze, Meshi's husband, fidgets as he changes from his suit into the pyjamas.

It is past midnight. Receding urban noise. Sustained hoot of an owl in the vicinage.

EFENZE

(Turning sharply towards the door. Heavy breathing.)
I said it.... I said it....

MESHI

(Raising her head from the pillow.)
What did you say, my dear husband?

EFENZE

Hem! The hour's come at last?

MESHI

The hour? What hour?
(Silence)
Come to bed, my dear, and have some rest.

EFENZE

(Efenze goes to bed, pulls the counterpane over himself, groans and tosses about. Owl hoots again.)
There's evil in the cry of that bird. It roots something out of my mind. What did she tell me again...? That

I've broken the oath and left her in the cold? She's been waiting for too long? That her husband will…will… O God, let me sleep for a while.
(Pause. Starts snoring, at first low then harsh and prolonged throttles.)

MESHI
(Pulling off the pillow beneath Efenze's head)
My dear…, my dear, you're not lying well.

EFENZE
Hei! Has he come already? *(Pause.)* Let him come plain if it's the hour.
(Pause.)
Let him come like seven vipers with seven fangs.
(Pause.)
Like seven witches and haunt and murder me.
(Pause.)
And Manka with them…. I loved Manka for His Excellency the Fool's money and not for Her Majesty the Harlot's love.
(Pause. Meshi begins to sob.)
Damn it. Let Sancheu's blood colour the River Mungo to the bottom at the sea…, mess up the slaughter house so that dogs can lap and smack and sing their masters hunting songs. Let Sancheu…Sancheu….

(Loud hoot of an owl. Efenze is startled. He screams, struggling to sit up in bed. Seeing Meshi sitting up he is scared, screams even louder. Meshi switches on the main lights.)

MESHI
(Sobbing.)
Oh, my husband! What's gone wrong with you? Always at this hour of the night!

EFENZE

(Pacific tone.)

What's the matter, ehn?

MESHI

My dear, tell me....Please, tell me what's eating you up.

(Pause.)

You vow you will never let me know, my dear husband.

EFENZE

(In a soft tone.)

What did you say, honey?

MESHI

What makes you scream with such horror in the night?

EFENZE

(In a lighter mood.)

Only a dream, my dear. Only a dream.

MESHI

Only a dream, Efe! You call this horrifying scream a dream?

EFENZE

I was only dreaming, Meshi.

MESHI

Efe, you can't deceive me anymore. Let me tell you straight. You've behaved strangely within these last six months. The same dream these last six months, my husband! Swearing evil spirits, invoking serpents, witches.... Many times you've talked carelessly and ceaselessly in your sleep, murmuring incantations, commanding blood to disappear into the valleys of dead hills. Many times you have leaped out of bed in fright, fleeing from your own dream like a monkey that flees from its own excrement. Many times you have raised neighbours in their sleep. And they have rushed here late in the night believing that someone in the house has given up life.

(Pause. Sobs.)

When I ask you, you dabble me like the morning dew and I forget about it.

(Pause.)

Many, many times you've forgotten that you share a bed with a wife. The woman you swore six years ago that she was the darling of your imagination.

(Pause.)

Those were the days, the sweet days that passed away like one joyful night.

(Weeps.)

My husband, I have known you to be a man of substance, a man of dignity, a prosperous politician. You used to tell me how you could auction all your tribe to own me. Just when I'm beginning to feel the pride of the wife of a prominent husband you have turned sour. Tell me darling, where have you destroyed your life?

EFENZE

(Brief laughter.)

Just a dream, my dear. There's nothing wrong.

MESHI

(Sternly.)

There is something seriously wrong with you, Efe. And you don't want to let me know. But there's something more than a dream. These last six months I have hardly seen the gentleman that I used to know.

(Sobs.)

O my god! Efe, you showed me paradise and you want to take it away again so soon.

EFENZE

(Laughs, then in a comforting tone.)

The road to paradise is very rough, Meshi. You are paradise itself. You don't know the obstacles I went through to marry you.

MESHI

Don't start playing those old tricks on me again.
(Pause.)

They used to be good when you were a happy young man in your bedroom. But your life has changed terribly. And I don't think I still possess you again. And you vow you will never tell me why, my husband.

EFENZE

I need some rest, even for thirty minutes. See, it's getting to 4 already.
(Pause)

Put off the main lights.

MESHI

Just tell me, EFe. Except you don't love me any more. Even if you don't, you should have some feeling for the children, especially the twins who are so fond of you.

EFENZE

I love you and care for the twins. Can I sleep now?

MESHI

I know you do, Efe. You used to. That was long ago. But I find feigned love in your eyes now. Especially, when you come home late in the night. I know some other loving woman is standing on my way. But I can't ask. How can I ask? Is there anything that can stop a man from tasting the outside world?

(Pause.)

I know some other woman is standing in the core of your heart. I don't want to know who she is.

(Pause)

But for the sake of the children I want to know your mind. I want to know whether you are safe or not.

EFENZE

(Heaves a prolonged sigh.)

Meshi, please let me go to sleep.

MESHI

Don't Efe, don't. I must know right away what is wrong with you. Many times you have warded off my concern with the matter, diverting to sweet talks.

(Clears a lump in her throat and starts sobbing.)

But I have to know. I must know now. You are dying, my husband, dying without saying a word. Oh God, how can I miss you so soon? Think about the twin. See how fondly they love you. How shall they live without you? Think about that, my husband and speak out your mind. Something can be done before it's too late. Efe, tell me what's killing you?

EFENZE

I know nothing.

MESHI

You know. The witch doctor at Kabaka said you know. He said that only you know the solution to your problem. And that there was no use skirting over the countryside troubling the sorcerers to reveal the cause

of what you know.
(With irritation)
Don't turn your back against me. Efe, turn and face me.
(Pause. Meshi sobs.)

EFENZE
Meshi, don't weep. There's nothing wrong yet.
(Pause.)

MESHI
(In a sob)
But something will be wrong. This night or tomorrow, this week or next month, even after one year! This strange behaviour of yours tells me so.
(Pause.)
Efe, who is that woman the native doctor at Kabaka said you should reconcile with before it was too late?

EFENZE
I don't know.
(Pause.)

MESHI
Why did your first wife leave you?

EFENZE
Because she wasn't my wife.

MESHI
She was. I have seen your marriage deed. And you have big children with her. The other one visited you last holiday and you lied that he was your brother's child.

EFENZE
His mother was not more my wife.

9

MESHI

Now you want to start turning me round and round again. I have been told that she suspected something terrible about you and left with her children.

EFENZE

And what's that?

MESHI

Anyway, let's not talk about that now. I want to know about the woman the witch doctor talked about. He said that the woman hated your former wife. That her husband is dead but still living in the air. And that you and his wife should perform a ritual on his grave or his spirit will do many things. I didn't understand what he meant by that. You refused to tell me after but I heard everything when he was whispering to you.

EFENZE

Our conversation was not meant for women to listen to.

MESHI

You were conversing about women. Efe please, tell me now. Who is this woman?

EFENZE

(Loud and harsh.)
A woman I know.

MESHI

A woman you know. Know how?

EFENZE

Like knowing the colour of blood.

MESHI

Hei! Efe, are you starting again?

EFENZE

(Indignant shuffling in the bed.)
It has just begun.

MESHI

What has just begun?

EFENZE

(Sits on the edge of the bed and stares Meshi in the face. With indignation)
The witch doctors...the sorcerers...the woman...the blood....

MESHI

(Sobbing.)
Efe, don't go away. Lie in the bed and tell me. Where does this woman live?

EFENZE

(Jumping out of bed and pacing about)
In the city.

MESHI

What part of the city?

EFENZE

Where drabbed bees meet to drink honey.

MESHI

Where's that?

EFENZE

At the junction of two grave yards.

11

MESHI

(Pertly.)

You are not speaking sense.

(Pause.)

How is the woman?

EFENZE

She's black. Her hair is black. Her skin is black. Her gown is black. Her soul is black...ever since her husband....Heii!

MESHI

(Sobbing in a low tone.)

Efe, where were you last evening?

EFENZE

With my wife.

MESHI

I don't mean me. I mean before you returned to me.

EFENZE

With my wife.

MESHI

Please, tell me where you were.

EFENZE

I went on a journey...to a place where there are no roads...only I know how to get there. And no one shall ever know....

(There's a knock offstage and a voice calls: "Mummy, Mervy and Austin are ready for school and the driver has come already.")

MESHI
Let me send the children to school.
(Footsteps are heard then a rustle of keys, footsteps, creaking sound of door being opened, bang of door as Meshi leaves bedchamber.)

EFENZE
(Fidgeting and groaning.)
We took the vow, but the vow is void. Why must blood run but in my head?
(Pause.)
It will run. Even now it's beginning to run. The money...where is the money? Blood will run.
(Pause then aloud.)
Hear, hear the feeble voice of conscience. A faint shadow of the mind that dies many times before its day.
(Pause.)
I took the vow....I did the deed. Let blood run now...now....You cannot eat eggs and want to lay them like a hen; cannot suck your child's breast like the giraffe; smell your mother's buttocks like the young he-goat.
(Meshi re-enters.)

MESHI
It's Ngando the driver. He has taken the children to school. I've asked him to call your friend Mr Wange on his way back. Tell me, Efe, who is Manka?

EFENZE
Heiii!

MESHI
Efe, who is Manka?

EFENZE
A woman.

MESHI

I know, but how is she related to you?

EFENZE

Why bother about the woman?

MESHI

You call her name often in your nightmares.
(Silence.)

Answer me, Efe. Who is this Manka?

EFE

(Loud enough to be heard out of the room.)

Let it run now...I mean now...so that I can sleep forever.
(Pitch rises.)

Let him say if I did it. The vow...what vow? Yes. I vowed to…to…. But was it I who did it?

(Paces the bedchamber, goes towards the wardrobe, scatters items in it, while Meshi breaks down to the floor, rises and kneels prostrate by the bed side, collects a pillow and buries her face in it sobbing. Efenze scatters more things violently and his voice grows louder.)

A man has a wife and doesn't make her proud....What man! She wanted me, Efe, Chairman of the Board of Directors of all government companies, a man of prominence at the centre of the country's politics.

(Crashes some oil vials on the floor, then paces round the bedchamber. Louder.)

Who was he, by the way? That slayer! That strangler who wanted to undercut me. How did he have his money, money enough to buy seven planets? How did he have it? Blood never rose in his head...

(Crashes objects against the wall.)

What man? What vow...what blood?

MESHI

I must know today where my feet stand in this life.

14

EFENZE

I had no say in the matter. I never closed his eyes, never wooed her. I was her man soon after. She sat on my knees and conjured heaven, we lavished quits along the Atlantic coast, sold the hotels and the lorries and the houses, churned arses in and out. And I sold out the contracts and did my investments. That's the game of life and you must be a juggler, if you want to live well. I became member of the central committee of the Pepper Soup Table and my greatest ambition now is to become member of the Political Bureau of the ruling party.

(Sitting on the floor, then aloud.)

Leave me alone, blank shadows of the mind. You prick me too late. You cannot now mend intestines poison has consumed. You cannot cure wounds ambitious daggers found their way through.

(Wange, a huge man in marked grassfield outfit enters followed by Ngando.)

WANGE

(Finding Efenze squatted wretchedly in a corner, pieces of broken bottles and other things like dresses, paper etc. scattered about the floor, exclaims.)

You see trouble! Monsieur le Directeur, is that where you are sitting now? On the floor, and with things broken and scattered about? Efe, my friend, have you gone so low?

MESHI

Mr Wange. Someone has dealt with your friend.

WANGE

Directeur! Ha, Directeur. PDG! Mister Efe, what's brought you so low? Talk for me, enh my friend.

15

(Pause.)

Hee...hee! Madam Efe, how did it start, enh? We were together last night but he wasn't like this. Hei...hei...heiii! Efe, talk for me. How did it start? What's happen?

MESHI

(Sobbing.)

Mr. Wange, your friend is done with. He's lost his mind and we'll soon lose all of him. That's why I sent for you. Oh, my husband, he's done with and he vows he will never let me know how. That's all about him.

(Sobs and beats about.)

WANGE

Madam, don't cry....

MESHI

I sent for you because I want you to take him to Kabaka to see his medicine man.

WANGE

Em...em....I have a serious business trip to make before ten o'clock this morning.

MESHI

What shall I do then? I can't go alone. I needed a responsible adult to go with. So I thought of you.

WANGE

I've to collect fifty million Francs for a contract today. I miss it today, that's all about it. I talk for him about it yesterday evening. Any how, let me see. I can send my land rover... No, my double-cabin stout. Kabaka is far away.

(Pause.)

16

O God, what can make big man turn this kind way?
Enh? What's make him turn this kind fool?
(Loudly.)
PDG! Directeur!
(Silence)
Chop I chop!
(Pause.)
That's you cannot even answer me? Your own friend!
Oh Efe!
(Pause.)
You have a beautiful woman, why are you treating
her this way, einh? Why don't you pity this woman,
this your beautiful woman and the children? Oh Efe!

EFENZE

My life is dark and you know why. I must grope in the
dark till my shadow denies its substance.
(Fidgeting with items in the suitcase.)
Here's a suit case filled with money. Take it. That's
money enough to buy seven planets.
(Falls asleep).

WANGE

There it is, my young man. It is the beginning to an
end. Only you know what's happened to you, not me.

MESHI

(Anxiously.)
You said you were together last night.

WANGE

Yes...yes...

MESHI

Where was that?

WANGE

Of course, at Mami Ndole. We were there drinking wine.

MESHI

Who owns the place?

WANGE

Of course, Mami Ndole.

MESHI

Does my husband have any problem with her?

WANGE

No. Who can have problem with big man to this extent?

(Pause.)

Let me see. Only with Manka....

(Efenze starts.)

Efe told me last night that he has big problem with Manka and that she has sworn that she will deal with Efe.

(Efenze starts again.)

But...But the problem can't get to this extent, of course. I think it's a small problem we can solve.

MESHI

Do you know this woman?

WANGE

Yes, of course, Mami Ndole, of course. Her real name is Manka.

MESHI

Who was her husband?

WANGE

Her husband was a very rich man. Richer than me and my friend put together. He was contractor for government companies where my friend, Efe is PDG. He build many houses in Europe and America. He build many, many houses in the country. He own many, many cars and a lot of money stacked in banks abroad and in the country.

MESHI

How did he have his money?

WANGE

He know how to play game with Monsieur le Directeur when it concern government contract. Only my friend former wife know them very, very well. It was because of Manka that his former wife, Talatu, went her away from my friend's home.

MESHI

What did she do to her?

WANGE

Ehm...! I don't know. I can't tell you. Only your husband can tell you.

MESHI

He doesn't tell me the truth. Efe is a different man from the one he made me think he was. O my God! When did the woman's husband die?

WANGE

Em...em...Manka's husband died a few years before you were married to Efe.

(Pauses.)

You cannot regret very much. You are still a beautiful young woman..., young beautiful woman. Sancheu was a very good friend of mine, very good friend with my friend, Efe...

(Efenze issues a loud scream, then swoons. Wange and Ngando rush towards Efenze and fan him.)

MESHI

(Screaming.)

Oooh, he' dead! My husband is dying!

(Sobbing.)

O Efe, you know the road to your grave and you won't say a word. You never said anything to me about it. What shall I do with the children without you? O, I have been living in deception, in illusion.

WANGE

(Mournfully.)

Sorry, sorry, my dear good friend, Efe. Who has done this kind of thing to my only dear friend?

MESHI

My husband hasn't slept a wink. He talked to himself the whole night, screaming in his dream....Mr Wange, you must show me where this woman lives.

WANGE

He lives near Balacot Quarter.

MESHI

Please, take me there so that I know the meaning of my life.

WANGE

I shall take you there but not today.

MESHI

When, Mr Wange?

WANGE

I'll tell you after.

MESHI

That woman must tell me about my husband's illness. She must know something about this strange behaviour of my husband. My husband calls her name every night these last six months...calls her name in his sleep...calls Manka, calls Sancheu and....

EFENZE

(Screams, carries his suitcase and rushes out of the stage.)
Let it run now...let it run right now. Now....now!

(Meshi runs after calling "Efe....Efe...."
followed by Wange and Ngando.)

ACT TWO

*In a luxurious sitting room in late Sancheu's house one week after.
The elegant pieces of furniture which have significantly depreciated
are carelessly displayed.*

It is morning.

*Manka, Sancheu's widow, is seated on a sofa on the rear wall,
deep in contemplation, her legs stretched out on the central table.*

*She has a fine statute, even though she appears unkempt. Her
hair ruffled and her black dress, although richly provided is not
suitably put on. She has several of necklaces round her neck and
bangles on her wrists.*

Wange, followed by Meshi, knocks and enters.

MANKA
(Screening their faces with contempt)

Ha! Is it you Mr Wange? What brings you to my house
this early morning?

WANGE

Just to greet you, Manka.

MANKA

Just to greet, Mr Wange? Is my medicine working
already? Ha, ha! I can tell from your looks.

WANGE

Manka, only greetings. We came to salute you.

MANKA

Thank you, Mr Wange. You thought about me after
many years. That's very kind of you. How's your
bosom friend, Efe? Is he still living?

WANGE

Still living, Manka. But....

MANKA

But what? Who's that came with you?

WANGE

(*Hesitatingly.*)
Madam Efe....

MANKA

(*Indignantly.*)
What? In my house? Out, viper! I don't like your face.
It wakes the ghosts in my nerves which your husband
duped me to kill. Go...go...go out of here.

MESHI

Madam, I will go. But let me know something from
you.

MANKA

I say out of my house, you hare.

MESHI

I want to know what you have done to my husband.
He calls only your name in his sleep. Now he is not
well.

MANKA

Go out of my house before I scratch out your eyes.
Your husband saved your life, so you want to save
his and I'd remain in the cold forever. Go...go.... Leave
my house, and let your womb be barren like the shell
of a crab.

MESHI

Madam….

MANKA

(Sternly.)

Leave my house before I pull out your womb. Leave…, leave my house….!

MESHI

I'm not leaving until you tell me what you've done to my husband.

MANKA

(Indignantly. Picks up a side stool.)

What? In my house? I'll yank off your head. Out, you hare.

WANGE

(Taking her out of the scene)

Madam, wait for me, you hear? Outside in the car across the road, you hear? She is angry say I brought you here. I remain here with her and she will talk for me what's happen to my friend Efe, you hear? And I make you know when I return. Hear me, Madam? You are a beautiful wife.

(Meshi sobs as she leaves the scene.)

Ha! Keep courage. Nothing wrong yet. If a monkey rejects banana, baboons will eat of course. Don't worry. I'd comfort you. I will help you. Only me can help you better, my dear.

(Exits Meshi.)

MANKA

You brought her to show me that gold can't rust, that poison can't kill her, that even a knife can't cut her flanks...ha...ha...ha...! You lie, Wange...ha...ha...ha...!

You see? Ehn...ehn...

(Pauses.)

How does Efe think I have been living? Tell me quick.... Is your friend dead? My medicine works. I know from your coming...ha...ha...ha...!

WANGE

Not dead, but he is not well. He is not correct in the head. He run wild. He living right now around the big, big garbage heap at the junction of two grave yards. O, sorry for my friend.

MANKA

Run wild? Hurray, Raphael Efe! Hurray, moneyman of the Central Committee! So he is dying?

WANGE

Dying and dying; swearing and swearing to kill any one who come near him.

MANKA

He's not yet dead? Sick in the head and not yet dead? A half fool is a complete fool, a complete fool a wise man. I never wanted him completely mad. I wanted him to know that he is mad and yet remember that he is a gallant gentleman, a prominent man in the central committee of the Country's People Democratic Murderers. That is the right way to kill a hare. Complete madness frees him from pains, from knowing pride.

WANGE

Why you go so far to do that to my friend, Manka?

MANKA

I followed your advice, Mr Wange. I went to Girimba, and I chose my medicine man. What else did you want?

WANGE

God of Tumukururu! Manka it's not me I tell you that, O!

MANKA

You told me to make him impotent.

WANGE

And you do different thing altogether.

MANKA

I chose my own method. I've despaired for all these years without a husband while Raphael Efe is living in the glory of my husband's death with a young wife. He too must die. I found an excellent wizard in Girimba. I'm happy his medicine works...ha...ha...ha...!

WANGE

But why you do that kind of thing to my friend, Manka?

MANKA

(Sternly.)

Do what? He deprived me of my husband, deprived me of my husband's wealth. Why did he do that? You too had your share of my husband's money. Didn't you? Speak, now? Am I lying? Ten million francs to keep your mouth shut!

WANGE

Please Manka, don't say that too loud.

MANKA

(Loud and hysterical.)

I'll say it, Wange. Am I lying? Didn't you take the money from my bloody hands? And your friend made me fall in love with him body and soul. And when our morning woke he abandoned me in the cold, on dew-covered fields. Why did he do that? Wange speak. Is your tongue tied? Tell me if I lie.

WANGE

Manka, you could have been patient just one time.

MANKA

What? Patient? How patient can you be, Wange, without a wife and without the abundant wealth your partner left? Patient? Patience is for those who still find value in life. Raphael Efe buried mine with my husband in the grave.

WANGE

Manka, help my friend, O! My friend is dying, O!

MANKA

Wange, don't put more steam in my anger. Efe loved me for my husband's money. The worst of it, he splashed mud on me one day and never said a word. My belly turned...my head turned...my mind turned. I asked myself: was this Efe who should be mine body and soul doing this to me; was this Efe whom I saved from going to prison after my husband's death, who was being charged for corruption and embezzlement of billions of francs, of state's funds? Not only that, his political rivals wanted his head at all cost. I saved him still. I had to work out a way to stop his name from being dragged in the mud. Mr Wange, is this my reward? Your friend Efe, has done a thing to me that tongues never can tell.

WANGE

Why you don't pity....

MANKA

Pity? I see how you pitied your friend by advising me to go to Girimba and make him impotent. So that you can own his wife behind his back. You men!

WANGE

(Agitating.)

No. How can you say that kind thing? I don't like that. I am an honest man. She is beautiful woman but...but I am honest man. The dog that looks after goats does not steal goats.

MANKA

Lies. You are no honest man, Wange. You men are the same, licking dishes with the back of your tongues and swearing with your back hands. You think all this finding out about your friend's illness is for nothing?

WANGE

For nothing, Manka.

MANKA

You took ten million francs from me and swore that you'd not reveal the cause of my husband's death. Now your friend is dying and you want to marry his wife. So that I shall remain in the cold forever.

WANGE

(Loud.)

No, Manka! Don't say that!

MANKA

You know Ralph and I were going to get married after the deed. He wanted to be the richest man in the country by combining my late husband's wealth and his. And I was to get married to him, to be the wife of the richest man and the most prominent politician in the country. But he never kept his vow. Ha...ha...ha...! My medicine works. Hurray, Raphael Efe! The python refused fewer legs because it thought it was bigger than the millipede and died having none. Ha...ha...! Efe denied second class to marry a queen. Ha... ha!

WANGE

But Manka, how can you save my friend? My friend is gone oooh! He's living on the garbage heap now, eating dirt and drinking urine. He wants to kill any one who talk for him or want to take him away.

MANKA

Let him murder his wife and marry Manka. That's all.

WANGE

But his first wife left him because of the deed.

MANKA

Efe didn't murder her. He pitied her and let her go. Instead of marrying me as he promised, married another woman. Now, my medicine works.

WANGE

Who can be this strong medicine man? Manka, how can I fit to see him?

MANKA

You must be mad yourself if you want to untie what has been tied firm. See who? The medicine man? Let

me advise you, Mr Wange. The tortoise lays eggs but
does not eat them. Because you eat eggs do not think
you can lay them. You'll never find the sorcerer. You
may comb the whole of Girimba but you will never
find him. Excellent sorcerer! He boils herbs in a
calabash.

WANGE

You've not done good, Manka. What kind of thing
have you done like this? Why you didn't let me know?

MANKA

Let you know! I couldn't. I don't trust men anymore.
Until I die, I can never trust them. I had to punish
Efe, to stop my husband's anger on me. He visits me
in my sleep, troubles me in my sleep since after his
death.

WANGE

(Worried.)
Your husband!

MANKA

Yes, my husband. A husband that was so kind-hearted,
so humble and hardworking.
(Sobs. Pause. Sobs.)
Manka! Manka! What did Manka want in this world
of plenty? Efe came into my life and took away all I
had – my heart, my soul, my body, my husband, my
wealth.... Gods of my ancestors! What did Manka
want in Sancheu's world of plenty?
(Shrieks. Sets about putting furniture in disorder. Shrieks louder.)
Heii! He has come again. Go...go....He comes even in
the day? This house is unsafe. I'll leave it to you.
Go...go... And because of his own ravenous greed
Raphael urged me on....Raphael Efenze! O, gods of

31

my ancestors, Raphael has done a thing too terrible to me that tongues cannot tell.

(Stares fixedly into space. Falls in a trance.)

Scene in the past. Sancheu's bedchamber after midnight. Sancheu is stretched out in the bed. He has a white jumper, a black pair of trousers and white socks on. Manka, cutely dressed and panicky, feels Sancheu's heartbeat with her palm.

MANKA

(Still panicking.)
    Cold!
(Tries to close Sancheu's eyelids.)
    Dead. Dead with his eyes open.
(Stoops under the bed and whispers.)
    Come out. He's dead. The potion worked. Very effective.
(Rising.)
    It worked.
(Efenze comes out of his hiding under the bed, dressed in suit.)
    Ralph, he's dead, dead with his eyes open....

EFENZE

(Examines Sancheu, turns toward Manka, in a whisper.)
    No...not yet dead....He's coming back to life.
(Puts the back of his hand on Sancheu's nose.)
    He is in a coma, but he's breathing again....
(Takes a head scarf close by and ties it round Sancheu's nose and mouth very firmly. Sancheu kicks and stretches till he is motionless.)

MANKA

(Shivering and whimpering. About to scream.)
    Dead. My husband dead....

EFENZE
(In a whisper as an owl cries on the heath.)
What next? We cannot take him to the river now. It's too early. Wrap him in the blanket. Cover those eyes. They look like sheep's eyes on a cloudy day.

MANKA
But if we go too late to the river we risk being attacked by armed robbers. Let's go now.

EFENZE
I think you are right. Come let's carry him to the boot of the car.

MANKA
Sssh! Don't shout. The children will wake. I drugged them with sleeping tablets a long time ago. Stab him first and let blood flow. So I can go to the police and tell them armed robbers ambushed him, ransacked the house, took money, property and his corpse away.
(Exits and returns with a knife. Handing the knife to Efenze.)
Stab him on his heart...on his head...on his thigh...everywhere....
(Efenze takes the knife but hesitates.)
Stab him. What, are you a woman? Stab the bastard!

EFENZE
(Shivering.)
No. let's stab him where we shall abandon him. No more the river. We leave him in a jungle not far away from here. So it would be thought thieves ambushed him on his way back. Appropriate place is where there are two grave yards. We throw him out near the car, stab him, abandon him and the car there. Get ready. Let's be going before his blood congeals. Remove the blanket on him. You shall follow me behind in your

own car and I'll drive him in his. I left mine far away from here. After we deposit him you will return home quick, quick and raise an alarm about his whereabouts.

MANKA
I won't sleep alone.

EFENZE
We shall discuss that hereafter. Get on. Remove the blanket. Put on his shoes.
(Manka hesitates, removes the blanket, puts on Sancheu's shoes, and assisted by Efenze, his body is borne out of the scene.)

Scene as before.

MANKA
You kept your promise, Mr Wange, not to tell any one because you had a lot of money to keep your mouth shut. Ten million francs to keep your mouth shut, Mr Wange.

WANGE
Please, don not speak so loud.

MANKA
Ten million francs! Why did you come nosing about my compound that night?

WANGE
Forget. That one that is past, think just now about my sick friend.

MANKA
You and your friend enriched yourselves and abandoned me. Why didn't you report to the police so that they could imprison me and set free my guilt?

WANGE

Manka, pity my friend and tell the sorcerer to cure him.

MANKA

Raphael Efe! Moneyman! Bigman of the Central Committee. He should be dead by now. Until he dies, I cannot sleep. An evil owl cries at the top of my roof every night. The sorcerer said it was my husband's spirit.

WANGE

Why? If the sorcerer, if he be strong make him punish the owl not my bossing friend Efe.

MANKA

What? Do away with the owl and leave Efe to continue with the glory of my husband's death? You are crazy. Is that what brought you here? Out of my house you viper!
(Throws flower vase at Wange)
I say out you murderer!

WANGE

Manka!

MANKA

Yes.

WANGE

Are you well in the head? See how you have wound my head. I came to see how I can fix the palaver with you and Efe but you have wound my head.

MANKA

You came too late.

WANGE

Too late how?

MANKA

The damage has been done. The charms cannot be softened. Sancheu's death cannot be reversed. Sancheu's death….. Hei! He's come again. Hei! Hei! H-e-i-i-i-i! Manka! Manka! What did Manka want in Sancheu's world of plenty?

(*Swoons in the sofa*)

WANGE

(*Confused and panicky*)
        Ha! What kind trouble is this? Manka! Manka!
(*Totters about the room wiping his forehead, then returns and sits near Manka on the sofa. Shaking her.*)
        Manka! Manka!

MANKA

(*Recovering*)
        Ah Mr Wange, are you the one?

WANGE

I am frightened. I fear that you are dead.

MANKA

Why? It was only a dream.

WANGE

For long, long time you no open your eyes and your mouth open. Believe me, I fear that you are dead.

MANKA

It was only a honeymoon dream. Ha, ha!
(Caressing Wange)
Mr Wange, you are very handsome, more handsome than before.

WANGE

No, Manka, don't do that.

MANKA

(Sends her hands round Wange's torso and grips him)
My dish has been cold for all these years. Can you make it warm, honey?

WANGE

(Struggling to liberate himself)
Not now....

MANKA

Come on, darling. Let it be now.

WANGE

No, no. Not now.

MANKA

I want it now.

WANGE

Please, don't do bad thing to me.

MANKA

Sweet heart, don't be afraid. I give it all to you.
(Tightening grip)
Take all of it.

WANGE

It's not good o, what you are doing please leave my body.

MANKA

Come on, honey. Do you have a wife to auction? I auctioned my husband many years ago. I will give it all to you if you auction your wife so that we can love forever.
(Squeezes Wange's balls).

WANGE

(Jumping from the sofa with a sharp cry)
Manka, why you do that? I come here to see how I can save my friend not to warm old dishes. Tell me how to get to the wizard at Girimba.

MANKA

Who, what? Let Efe murder his wife and marry me or he shall die in pain.

WANGE

He can't do nothing now. He is sick in the head.

MANKA

Tell him to murder his wife as I murdered my husband. O Sancheu...Sancheu! Who would have known the value of a dog's tail when it was still hanging there? My husband, forgive me... Hei! He's come. He's come. Wange leave my house. Leave my parlour now. Out, you viper! I say, out! Murderer, I say out of my parlour!
(Throws an object that lands on Wange's head)

WANGE

(Loud, amidst a commotion of feet and moving objects.)
Manka! Hoi, she has broken my head, oooh!

MANKA

I say out of my house!
(Throws a bottle which crashes near Wange)

WANGE

Ha! What kind trouble is this? What kind thing is
turning in my eyes like this?

MANKA

You killed my husband. Now you want... you want
stale food. Out! Out!
(Throws more objects at Wange.)

WANGE

(Loud.)
Manka! Manka! I'm leaving your house. I'm leaving
ooooh! Don't split my head.

MANKA

I lost my head and murdered Sancheu....Heii! He's
here again...
(Throws another object at Wange)

WANGE

(Screaming as he leaves the house)
Manka, don't kill me. I am going.

MANKA

(Tosses furniture about.)
I cannot sleep any more... I'll leave him forever. I'll
leave his house...I can't stay here any longer. Let him
stay in his house alone....Let him bring all the owls in
the world and they live in his house.
(Screaming and setting furniture in disorder.)
My husband's blood will climb in your heads. I have
been waiting for too long. For too long. Waiting for

39

Efe to kill his wife and marry me. I'm going to face him at the junction of two grave yards.

(As she exits house)

I am going to bring the police, let them see him stabbing my husband, stabbing Sancheu near two grave yards.

(Voice fades.)

ACT THREE

Late afternoon.

Besides a garbage heap. Manka rummages the heap. There is noise made by her bangles and necklaces as she searches.

MANKA

(Singing.)

Nde lata Njinju	(I deceived Njinju
Njinju a goh egi nfet	Njinjuh caught his mother and ate
Ndog ageh nguoh legala ruli	I hid mine
Nyig lo oooh!	In the armpit of a stone oooh!)

(Stops singing.)

My mother told me the story.... It was the hare that deceived Njinju, the lion. A cunning hare! The lion and the hare, two good friends in the forest, decided to kill their mothers in order to survive the famine. The hare told the lion; "Let's kill your mother first. My mother is sick. Hares don't taste good when they are sick. And the lion, greedy lion, killed his mother and both feasted on the meat for days. The lion... foolish thing... that would kill his own mother and eat... When the meat was finished the lion told the hare; "Friend, it is your own turn now. Let's kill your mother and eat." The hare told the lion: "Go into the forest and look for wood while I will kill and bring back my mother". When the lion left, the hare filled the pot with plantain pulps and put it on the fire. The lion returned with a mighty bundle of wood, tired and hungry. Then said the hare: "Now I am going to look for pepper. Don't open the pot yet. If you do so when it is not yet ready the meat will turn to plantain pulps." And the hare went out and hid in a corner and watched the hungry lion open the lid of the pot to take a look at the quantity of meat. But what did it see? Plantain pulps. "See, you foolish lion," said the hare. "I warned you not to open the pot. Now we have lost our good meal because you are always impatient, always very hungry. We are both going to starve, but first, you must find me food to eat today. And so the hare went into the cave to eat with his mother every day while the lion was dying of hunger. One day the lion followed him closely behind until the hare reached the mouth of the cave. After eating the hare came out with its mother and sat on a rock and started singing:

Nde lata Njinju	(I deceived Njinju
Njinju a goh egi nfet	Njinjuh caught his mother and ate
Ndog ageh nguoh legala ruli	I hid mine
Nyig lo oooh!	In the armpit of a stone oooh!)

(Stops singing.)

The lion pounced on the hare's mother and ate her all alone....Fine...that was good...how should the hare be so clever... Life has so many traps for clever people and so many too for foolish ones.

(Efenze comes in unnoticed carrying a suitcase. Laughs heartily.)

What are you doing here? Viper, go...go you cunning hare! What do you want in my home, enh! Have you killed your own mother? Can we eat her meat now. I killed mine long ago and we ate her together. You

refused to kill yours. Go... go... away from here... go,
viper!
(Chases Efenze round the heap.)
You will kill your mother today. What? Ungrateful
hare, lion...viper...owl!

EFENZE
(Efenze stops and rummages the heap)
See. My beautiful bracelet. I found it on the heap.
Hi...hi...hi...!

MANKA
Give me it. It's mine.

EFENZE
It's mine. It's me who found it. It's mine...

MANKA
I say give it to me.

EFENZE
No.

They quarrel at high pitch.

MANKA
I say give it to me, you murderer.

EFENZE
Thief, you want to rob me.

MANKA
Murderer of mothers!

EFENZE

It's mine. I found it.

MANKA

What wickedness!

EFENZE

Ya...ya...woo...woo!

MANKA

Ya, too. What were you doing at the junction of two grave yards?

EFENZE

Ya... eh! A rogue climbing palm trees like an ape, scratching your bottoms and smelling your fingers.

MANKA

I was in Girimba and saw the man who killed my husband.

EFENZE

Ya...ya...are you not ashamed?

MANKA

You will give me back that husband...hare...viper!

EFENZE

You will die...ya...ya!

MANKA

I say give me my bracelet. It's my husband's money. *(Pause.)*
Yes...you see...yes, enhenh...enhenh....

EFENZE

A dog would eat his tail and think that he can whisk off flies with teeth. Ya...woo...woo...

MANKA

You are a wizard. Yes, you see...you see...enhehn...enhehn....

EFENZE

I offer it to you.

MANKA

My fine bracelet! My beautiful gold bracelet! Efe, my dear, help me to put it on.

(Efenze struggles to put the bracelet on Manka's wrist.)

My nice, beautiful bracelet! Hi...hi...!

(Pause)

EFENZE

(Surprised tone.)

Manka, see!

MANKA

Who's that?

EFENZE

Is he a ghost or an owl?

MANKA

(Frightened tone)

A ghost.... Sancheu's ghost. Heiii!

EFENZE

Who are you? An owl, a ghost?

NGANDO

Oga, I'm not a ghost. I am Ngando, your driver. *(Pause.)*

EFENZE

He looks familiar. I have seen him on earth....When did you go mad?

NGANDO

I'm not mad, Oga. I've come to tell you that your wife, Meshi is dead.

EFENZE

Who....what has what....?

NGANDO

Your wife, Meshi. She is dead.

EFENZE

How can she die? Before I went on this mission I left her with a lot of money. Money enough to buy seven planets!

NGANDO

She has committed suicide.

EFENZE

How? Who?

NGANDO

Your wife, Meshi. Your friend, Mr Wange, said he would marry her. Being truthful to herself, she refused. Mr Wange drugged her and raped her. When Madam got back to her senses and discovered the dreadful thing done to her by your friend she drank some liquid, the kind I can't tell and started wailing and vomiting blood. When I got to her room it was too late. She was kicking and groaning. The last words I heard her utter were "What men, what world!" And that was her end.

EFENZE

Go and advise her to return to the world. Knock at the doors of the safe till money shrieks in the coffin and wake her from sleep. Play drums, drink and eat swine and sweat till the burning fats kindle her to life. Go to the Central Committee and collect the money for the contracts I had signed. There's a lot of it there. Take it to Kabaka and tell the marabou to secure my post of the President of the Board of Directors of all the government companies. Let no one take it, especially my political opponents. I am on mission and will be back soon to become a member of the Political Bureau.

NGANDO

Please, Oga, come back home. The twins can't survive without you. Since Madam died they have been a worry. Always asking: Where is Mama? Where is Papa?

MANKA

(Hysterically.)
Go...go...viper, devil from Girimba, ghost, owl....

EFENZE

(Threateningly.)
Go, cricket, member of the Country's People Democratic Murderers. Go and sweat on your ankles and on your knees. Go...go...go....
(Runs after Ngando throwing stones.)

NGANDO

(Fleeing.)
>Hoii! They have killed me with stones.

MANKA

>O, my beautiful darling bracelet!

EFENZE

(Returning)
>That's for your wedding.

MANKA

>For my wedding?

EFENZE

(Excited pitch)
>Hi...hi...hi...! Will you marry me? Come...come on, young man. Come and marry me. Come, my sweet husband.
(Spreading her arms)
>Come, come right here.

EFENZE

>Not now.

MANKA

(Holding Efenze's hand)
>Come honey, don't be ashamed. I am the queen offered by nature into your arms.

EFENZE

>Tell me. What do you want?

MANKA

>Confess your love for me.

EFENZE

(Holding Manka's other hand)

  Listen then. Manka, Manka! Queen of the Universe! On this solemn altar, I do confess my love for you. Like the rain nurtures the soil, like the moon lights the earth at midnight, like the sun heats the bodies at noon, like the breeze fondles the leaves of trees, let her soul feel mine, touch mine, nurture mine, fondle mine, knowing her in no other name but "wife". To you, sacred eye of Day, Minister of my bridal professing, let you be my witness. Let you be my witness in the womb of the earth, in the shadows of the sky when cocks' voices are thrilled by evil spirits. You have to travel to Kabaka like a thief to bring back life stolen by corpses living in the underworld, corpses without fangs that must be hanged on a withered tree in the forest until their souls visit Girimba to....

MANKA

(Cutting in.)

  To you, Princess of the Night, pampering daughter of the Universe. Like the night woos the day, like the seas beckon the rivers, like sugar melts in water, let my husband's soul, woo mine, beckon mine, melt with mine into one, till the watchful eye of the star falls on a stone, and I shall call him no other name but "husband". You, solemn moon, are witness of my protestation. Here, on this sacred altar, I swear my life for my husband. Ours is the call of blood, and body and soul.

(They embrace, looking into each other's eyes for a moment. Wange enters at the far end of the stage unnoticed. Manka pushes Efenze away.)

  Leave me. Why are you pressing me so hard?

(She picks a big stick and hits on Efenze's head.)

EFENZE

(Shrieks and rubs his head with both hands)
A mad woman has broken my head.
(Squats on the ground and rubs his head.)

MANKA

(Advancing towards Efenze and threatening to hit him again.)
You are a mad man.
(Turns away and grins)
Yes...you see? Yes, enhehn...enhenh!

EFENZE

(Pointing at her)
You are mad, you are a mad woman.

MANKA

(As she turns towards Efenze she sees Wange crawling on his belly to snatch the suitcase from Efenze.)
Heii! That owl has come again, that viper. They will never leave me in peace in this house. They will never leave me in peace. Go...go...
(Throws the stick at Wange)

EFENZE

(Rising)
What are you doing here again?

WANGE

Your wife is dead. And I want the keys of your safe to prepare her funeral...and...cure the twins....They too may not live long. Give me the key of the safe.

EFENZE

(Searching about as if for a stick or stone. Stops, then swearing as he runs muscularly after Wange who flees from the scene.)
Go and lick the buttock of a pig. You swine.

50

(Returning)

If crabs have holes then those who see them, see them only in the night....Only those who know the holes can put in them what things they want. A ratmole jumps over the fence in the day and sits on a rock staring at you in the face. You think you are friends because it is watching you but it sees nowhere. It can only see the night. The day for him is dark like the deepest bottom of a pit.

(Squats on the ground still rubbing his head. Manka squats behind him stretching her legs to his sides, starts splitting his hair to look for lice.)

EFENZE

(Opens his suitcase and brings out a card. Giving it behind to Manka.)

That is my Central Committee card.

(Manka takes it, examines, smiles, throws it back to Efenze and continues searching for lies on his head.)

The card is a passport to every place in the land. We can cross seven rivers, go underground in the world of the spirits, walk along the mountain tops, fly into the valleys and no one would stand on our way.

(Puts the card back in the suitcase, closes and puts it aside. He takes a rusty piece of metal and scrubs Manka's toe-nails.)

It's nice to be a member of the Central Committee of the Pepper Soup Table. Every person there is Bigman. But most are traitors, swindlers, murderers, rogues of unprecedented match. You eat food there but you don't know where it comes from. They give you money, you do not know where it comes from. You ride in cars which look like those which carry corpses to the underworld. You do not know where they come from. But there is big trouble there. We cannot go there. Raw meat is almost finished in the cans of the palace. Though we have a passport for the Central

51

Committee we shall go elsewhere...where there are mightier animals with decent and softer flesh...where....

MANKA

Did you see my shadow there?

EFENZE

No, only dead women whose souls are put in a coffin and their bodies are devoured by the murderers, women whose heads have been pounded with the buttocks of guns by the murderers.

MANKA

I will not go there. My shadow will be imprisoned in a coffin and they will come and sing strange things in my ears. We can go to strange countries across the mountains and the rivers, across the forests and the grass fields, sailing in the clouds, and we can go to night club beyond those horizons were the sun is setting and dance to our fill. Do you know how to dance? Do you dance Makossa?

EFENZE

Yes, very well. I dance well when the clock bird tunes an enchanting song and the woodpecker pecks the guitar on the dry wood and Lebialem Falls beat the drums on ancient rocks. That's when I'm touched with melody.

MANKA

Lies, you don't know how to dance.
(Laughs provocatively, rises and dances as she sings.)

Na me and you today
Na me and you today, today
Them been want for qua my massa
Na me and he today o-o-o-h
Na me and he today, today....

Caught in the rhythm of the song, Efenze rises and dances too. Both Manka and himself strut in odd choreographic patterns. Manka stops dancing but continues to sing and nod her head in admiration for Efenze's crazy, disorderly but concentrated struts. She stops singing and laughs fitfully at Efenze who continues to dance even when the singing has stopped. Efenze chases her round the mound, throwing stones and sticks at her. Manka too throws things at him. Wange crawls stealthily towards the refuse mound, his hand stretched toward Efenze's suitcase.

MANKA

(As she yells and turns to run away she sees Wange.)
    Heii, viper! What have you come again to do?
(Wange, in attempt to skip backwards slides and falls.)

EFENZE

(Reaches him and with a big stick hits Wange on the head. Wange swoons. As both Efenze and Manka continue to pound on him with sticks.)
    Hold, rogue! Hold, thief of the Central Committee.
    Wants to steal my suitcase. Hoii! Let me see any of
    them here again. I will season his skull with stones.

MANKA

(Retreating)
    Hei! He's dead.

EFENZE

(Retreating too.)
     Hunh! Can a lion die?
(Both stare at Wange as he crawls distressingly out of the stage. Efenze returns and collects his suitcase, opens it and examines the papers inside, item after item, while Manka searches the rubbish heap.)

MANKA

(Returning with a piece of stale bread and sitting near Efenze. With excitement.)
     I have found a beautiful cake. Here, my darling is a
     piece of cake for you
(Putting a piece in Efenze's mouth. Efenze munches. She puts some in Efenze's mouth, then holds her in his arms.)
     This, darling, is your wedding cake, hi...hi...hi...!

EFENZE

Hehm! Tastes good. Where did you find it?

MANKA

On the heap. Come, darling. Eat more of the cake.

EFENZE

I'll eat all of it.

MANKA

Eat all of it. It's for the best of our marriage. Till the moon shall strain its sight in guarding us.
(Both giggle.)

EFENZE

Till all the honey in the moon has been sucked by us.

MANKA

Till the night has fled and left the stars in the eye of
the day.
(In a soft spoken-tone.)
Come, my dear, let me tell you something.

EFENZE

No.

MANKA

Come on, young man, come on.... Hi..hi..hi...! Come on.

EFENZE

I'll not come.

MANKA

Come love, come lets... let's make... let's....
(Grabs Efenze on the groins)

EFENZE

(Skipping to his feet with a sharp cry and holding his groins)
Hoi! You have cracked my balls.

MANKA

(In a soft spoken-tone.)
Come, my dear, let me tell you something
(Efenze writhes with pain and shakes his head in objection.)
Come on, young man, come on.
(Beckons Efenze, a wry smile on her face.)

EFENZE

*(Moving cautiously towards Manka, still holding his groins. Manka
stretches her hand to hold him. Retreating.)*
No, I will not come. You have cracked my balls.
*(Manka rises and follows him round the mound. Efenze stops at a
point. Manka reaches him, they fight and scream. Efenze throws*

Manka on the ground, presses her with one hand and with the other he starts pulling down his trousers. Lights fade. Blackout for almost twenty seconds, while amorous cries are heard in the background of the stage. Light glows again and reveals Efenze and Manka rising from the ground and adjusting their dresses. Efenze wipes his face, adjusts his trousers and looks about in astonishment.)
Where is this? Am I Efenze?
(Pinches himself hard on the thigh)

MANKA
How did we get here to the rubbish heap?

EFENZE
(Astonished.)
Manka, where is this? Am I Efenze?

MANKA
(Also astonished)
How did we get to this rubbish dump?

EFENZE
O, I shall kill myself...I shall run mad. Who cast the spell on me?
(Pause.)
Manka, have I been dreaming?
(Silence. They look at each other in total bewilderment.)

MANKA
(Weeping)
We are being punished.

EFENZE
Punished?

MANKA

O, why did I do it? Why...why...why...? Am I the pig that spent its life digging for wealth and ended up in the filthy sty? Is this me, Manka, the charm of young men? What would they say I wanted in this world when I had enough? O Sancheu...my husband, calm your fury. Forgive me my husband. It was all my fault.

EFENZE

I can't stand the shame anymore. I will kill myself.
(Searches round the heap and discovers a rusty dagger.)
I will stab myself. It's not me Raphael Efenze to go back to the society of men. I shall not become the laughing stock of those who envied me.

MANKA

And what will I do?

EFENZE

Kill yourself too if you want to. For me this is my end.
(Raises knife to stab himself. Owl hoots very loud. Efenze startles and looks about.)

MANKA

(Manka picks a stick and hits on Efenze's head.)
It is this owl who brought me to the junction of seven wizards.

EFENZE

Ya! Animal without bones. Hen without feathers. Cockroach without wings. Ya!

MANKA

(Chasing Efenze round the heap.)
Man-eater. Where did you keep my husband? You fool who denied the crab and ate the soup. And I shall go

to Girimba to boil you in a calabash. You are the fool.
Ehn...you see? I must doctor you in Girimba.

(Efenze stops and both of them struggle. Tired, Manka retires close to the heap, squats, folds her arms.)

This is my home. I shall never go anywhere to meet wizards like this one.

(She bows her head as though in contemplation. Efenze too moves slowly and squats on another end of the heap staring fixedly into space.)

MANKA

(Weeping)
It's the call.

EFENZE

I'll kill myself.

MANKA

Kill me first?

EFENZE

Here's a dagger. I'll stab myself. And after you'll do same.

MANKA

No. Stab me first and after stab yourself.

EFENZE

Kill yourself if you want to. For me this is my end. O God, give me the courage. And now Manka, I'll see you no more.

MANKA

O, no. Don't leave me alone.

EFENZE

Farewell, Manka…

MANKA

(Screaming)
Do-o-o-o-n't.
(Owl hoots. Efenze shrieks.)

EFENZE

Let blood run now. Let it run now into valleys without slopes.

MANKA

(Owl hoots very loud)
Here he comes again.

EFENZE

You Manka brought me to the junction of grave yards. I can't stay here anymore. I'm going. I'm going to the two grave yards. Going to the two grave yards....
(His voice fades as he exits.)

MANKA

(Going after him)
Man-eater. Where did you keep my husband? You fool, that denied the crab and ate its soup. Come back and tell me where you kept my husband. Come back, mad man and tell me where you kept my husband.

(Exits)